# Effective Business Plan

Practical Guide to Creating an Excellent Business Plan that Attracts Funding to Turn Your Ideas into a Successful Business

A. Luvaren

Copyright © 2024

# Practical Guide

# 1. Introduction

In the modern economic landscape, characterized by rapid changes and increasing competition, business planning has become a fundamental element for the success of any enterprise. Creating a business plan is one of the first and most important activities that an entrepreneur must undertake. A business plan is not just a formal document, but a strategic guide that outlines the company's objectives, necessary resources, marketing strategies, and financial projections. It is a tool that helps define the company's direction and maintain focus on its priorities, while also providing a solid foundation for making informed decisions.

### What is a Business Plan

A business plan is a written document that describes in detail how an existing or new company will achieve its goals. The business plan serves several functions, including defining the company vision, resource planning, marketing strategy, and forecasting financial results. Typically, a business plan includes:

1. **Executive Summary**: A concise overview of the business project, highlighting the key points of the plan.

2. **Company Description**: Detailed information about the company, including its mission, vision, organizational structure, and company history.

3. **Market Analysis**: An evaluation of the target market, including size, customer segments, market trends, and competitive analysis.

4. **Organization and Management**: The company's organizational structure and the profiles of the management team.

5. **Products or Services**: Detailed descriptions of the products or services offered by the company.

6. **Marketing and Sales Strategy**: A plan for promoting and selling the products or

services, including pricing, distribution, and promotional strategies.

7. **Funding Request**: If the company is seeking external funding, this section details the amount requested and the plans for using the funds.

8. **Financial Projections**: Short and long-term financial forecasts, including balance sheets, income statements, and cash flow statements.

9. **Appendices**: Additional documents supporting the plan, such as team members' resumes, detailed market research, etc.

### The Importance of an Effective Business Plan

#### Strategic Guide

An effective business plan serves as a roadmap for the company, outlining strategies to achieve the set goals. This helps entrepreneurs stay on course and avoid distractions that may deviate the company from its main objectives.

#### Performance Evaluation and Monitoring

Through a well-structured business plan, clear and measurable performance indicators can be established. This allows entrepreneurs to monitor the company's progress against the set goals and make necessary adjustments.

#### Communication Tool

The business plan is also a fundamental communication tool, both internally and externally. Internally, it helps team members understand the company's vision and work towards common goals. Externally, it can be used to communicate with potential investors, business partners, and other stakeholders, providing a clear understanding of the opportunities and risks associated with the business.

#### Attracting Funding

For startups and growing businesses, the business plan is often indispensable for attracting funding. Investors and financial institutions require a detailed business plan to assess the feasibility and profitability of the business project. A well-prepared plan increases the company's credibility and can make the difference in the decision to finance the business or not.

#### Resource Planning

An effective business plan also aids in the planning and allocation of company resources. By identifying the necessary resources – financial, human, and material – in advance, the company can better plan its operations and reduce the risk of shortages or surpluses.

#### Risk Management

The process of drafting a business plan

requires a thorough assessment of potential risks and strategies to mitigate them. This helps the company prepare for challenges and develop contingency plans to address unforeseen events.

A business plan is not just a formal document required to secure funding; it is an essential tool for the strategic and operational planning of a company. It helps clarify the company's vision, set realistic goals, and plan the necessary resources to achieve them. Additionally, it facilitates communication with internal and external stakeholders and provides a basis for evaluating and monitoring business performance. In summary, an effective business plan is crucial for the long-term success of any enterprise, providing clear direction and helping navigate through market uncertainties and challenges.

## 2. Fundamentals of the Business Plan

A business plan is much more than a simple document; it is the strategic map that guides a company towards success. Creating a business plan requires a deep understanding of your business, the market you operate in, and the resources needed to achieve your goals. A well-crafted business plan helps clarify the business vision, establish concrete objectives, and develop strategies to achieve them.

### Definition of a Business Plan

A business plan is a formal document that details a company's goals, the strategies to achieve them, and the resource requirements. It is used both for internal planning and for communication with investors, partners, and other stakeholders. Its main function is to provide a clear and structured vision of the business, including financial forecasts, market analysis, marketing strategy, and organizational structure.

# General Structure of a Business Plan

An effective business plan is structured into several key sections that cover all essential aspects of the business activity. The general structure of a business plan can vary slightly depending on the type of business and the target audience, but it generally includes the following components:

1. **Executive Summary**

   - **Project Description**: Brief overview of the company and its objectives.

   - **Mission and Vision**: Company mission and vision statement.

   - **Products or Services**: Brief description of the products or services offered.

   - **Key Financial Information**: Overview of the main financial projections.

   - **Funding Request**: If applicable, the amount of funding requested and intended use.

2. **Company Description**

   - **Company History**: Background of the company and the motivation for its founding.

   - **Legal Structure**: Legal form of the company (e.g., LLC, corporation).

   - **Location**: Company headquarters and any other operational locations.

   - **Ownership and Governance**: Information about the owners and the governance structure.


3. **Market Analysis**

   - **Market Description**: Analysis of the target sector, including size and growth trends.

   - **Market Segmentation**: Identification of different target customer segments.

   - **Competitive Analysis**: Evaluation of main competitors and their positioning.

   - **Market Demand**: Projections of the demand for the products or services offered.

4. **Organization and Management**

   - **Organizational Structure**: Organizational chart and description of main business functions.

   - **Management Team**: Profiles of key management team members and their competencies.

   - **Hiring Plans**: Strategy for hiring new staff and developing skills.


5. **Products or Services**

   - **Product/Service Description**: Details about the products or services offered, including features and benefits.

   - **Product Life Cycle**: Information on the development status and product life cycle.

   - **Research and Development**: Plans and budget for research and development of new products or improvements.


6. **Marketing and Sales Strategy**

- **Marketing Strategy**: Overview of marketing strategies, including positioning, pricing, promotion, and distribution.

- **Sales Plan**: Strategy for selling products or services, including the sales process and distribution channels.

- **SWOT Analysis**: Identification of strengths, weaknesses, opportunities, and threats.

7. **Funding Request**

- **Amount Requested**: Details about the amount of funding needed.

- **Use of Funds**: Description of how the requested funds will be used.

- **Repayment Strategy**: If applicable, plan for repaying the funding.

8. **Financial Projections**

- **Income Statement**: Projections of revenues and expenses.

- **Balance Sheet**: Expected financial position.

   - **Cash Flow Statement**: Projections of operational, financial, and investment cash flows.

   - **Break-Even Analysis**: Calculation of the break-even point and related considerations.

9. **Appendices**

   - **Supporting Documentation**: Resumes of the management team, detailed market research, key contracts, legal agreements, etc.

### Types of Business Plans

Business plans can vary significantly based on their purpose. Here are some of the most common types:

1. **Start-Up Business Plan**

- **Purpose**: Used by new businesses to outline the initial path, attract investors, and obtain funding.

- **Features**: Includes a detailed description of the product or service, market analysis, financial projections, and marketing plans.


2. **Internal Business Plan**

- **Purpose**: Used within the company to plan and monitor specific projects or the expansion of new products or services.

- **Features**: Greater emphasis on operational strategies and implementation details compared to financial projections.


3. **Strategic Business Plan**

- **Purpose**: A long-term planning tool that defines the company's strategic objectives and the actions needed to achieve them.

- **Features**: Includes a high-level vision, long-term goals, SWOT analysis, and strategic plans.

4. **Operational Business Plan**

   - **Purpose**: Focused on daily operations and operational efficiency.

   - **Features**: Details operational processes, necessary resources, and key performance indicators (KPIs) to measure effectiveness.


5. **Growth Business Plan**

   - **Purpose**: Used by established companies seeking expansion, either through new markets, new products, or acquisitions.

   - **Features**: Detailed analysis of growth opportunities, resource requirements, and marketing strategies.


6. **Feasibility Business Plan**

   - **Purpose**: Used to assess the feasibility of a new business idea or project.

   - **Features**: Includes market analysis, risk assessment, and financial projections to determine the project's viability.

7. **Loan Business Plan**

   - **Purpose**: Specifically created to obtain a loan from a bank or other financial institution.

   - **Features**: Includes a detailed funding request, repayment plans, and offered collateral.

The business plan is a vital tool for any company, regardless of its stage in the life cycle. Whether it is a start-up seeking funding, an established company planning a new expansion, or a business looking to improve internal operations, a well-crafted business plan is essential for success. Understanding the fundamentals of a business plan, its general structure, and the different types available allows entrepreneurs to create effective documents that guide the company towards achieving its goals.

# 3. Market Analysis in the Business Plan

Market analysis is a crucial component of the business plan that provides a detailed overview of the industry in which the company operates. It helps to better understand the competitive environment, identify growth opportunities, and mitigate risks. Market analysis comprises several sections, including market research, target customer identification, competitor analysis, and the evaluation of opportunities and threats in the market.

### Market Research

Market research is the process of collecting and analyzing information related to the market in which you operate. It provides essential data on customers, competitors, and industry trends, enabling the company to make informed decisions. There are two main types of market research:

1. **Primary Market Research**

   - **Methods**: Includes surveys, interviews, focus groups, and direct observations.

   - **Objectives**: Gathering data directly from consumers to understand their preferences, needs, and behaviors.

   - **Advantages**: Provides specific and detailed information about the target audience.


2. **Secondary Market Research**

   - **Methods**: Analysis of existing data such as industry reports, published market studies, specialized journal articles, and government data.

   - **Objectives**: Obtain an overview of the market and current trends.

   - **Advantages**: Less costly and time-consuming than primary research.


The combination of primary and secondary research provides a solid information base for market analysis, allowing the development of more effective and targeted strategies.

### Identification of Target Customers

Identifying the target customers is fundamental for developing products, services, and marketing strategies that meet specific consumer needs. This process includes several steps:

1. **Market Segmentation**

   - **Definition**: Dividing the total market into groups of consumers with similar characteristics.

   - **Segmentation Criteria**: Demographic (age, gender, income), geographic (location), psychographic (lifestyle, personality), behavioral (purchase habits, brand loyalty).

   - **Objectives**: Identify specific market segments that can be served more effectively by the company.

2. **Ideal Customer Profiling**

   - **Description**: Creating a detailed profile of the ideal customer for each market segment.

   - **Elements**: Demographic data, needs and desires, purchase behavior, preferred communication channels.

   - **Advantages**: Improves the company's ability to create personalized marketing messages and develop products that better meet customer needs.


3. **Customer Needs Analysis**

   - **Methods**: Surveys, interviews, customer feedback analysis.

   - **Objectives**: Understand customers' needs, expectations, and problems.

   - **Advantages**: Allows the company to tailor its offerings to better meet market expectations.

### Competitor Analysis

Competitor analysis is an essential component of the business plan that helps to understand competitors' positioning and identify opportunities and threats arising from the presence of other companies in the market. This analysis includes several key elements:

1. **Identification of Major Competitors**

   - **Definition**: Identifying companies that offer similar products or services.

   - **Methods**: Market research, direct observations, industry report analysis.

2. **Evaluation of Strengths and Weaknesses**

   - **SWOT Analysis**: Analysis of each competitor's strengths, weaknesses, opportunities, and threats.

   - **Objectives**: Understand competitors' capabilities and identify areas where the company can differentiate itself.

3. **Analysis of Marketing and Sales Strategies**

   - **Elements**: Study of competitors' pricing, promotion, distribution, and positioning strategies.

   - **Advantages**: Allows identification of successful competitors' tactics and adaptation of one's own strategies accordingly.

4. **Market Share Evaluation**

   - **Definition**: Analysis of the market share held by each competitor.

   - **Methods**: Sales data, industry reports.

   - **Objectives**: Understand the company's relative position in the market and identify areas of potential growth.

5. **Benchmarking**

   - **Definition**: Comparison of the

company's performance with that of major competitors.

  - **Elements**: Key performance indicators (KPIs) such as profitability, operational efficiency, customer satisfaction.

  - **Advantages**: Identifies industry best practices and helps improve one's own operations.

### Market Opportunities and Threats

The analysis of opportunities and threats is a crucial element for understanding market dynamics and developing strategies that can leverage emerging opportunities and mitigate risks. This process is based on several activities:

1. **Identification of Opportunities**

  - **New Market Trends**: Study of emerging trends that can represent new growth opportunities.

- **Unmet Customer Needs**: Analysis of market gaps that the company can fill with its products or services.

 - **Technological Innovations**: Evaluation of new technologies that can be used to improve products or business processes.

 - **Geographic Expansion**: Identification of new geographic markets that the company can explore.


2. **Evaluation of Threats**

 - **Regulatory Changes**: Monitoring changes in regulations that can affect business operations.

 - **Competitive Evolution**: Analysis of competitors' strategic moves that can pose a threat.

 - **Economic Risks**: Evaluation of general economic conditions that can affect product or service demand.

 - **Technological Risks**: Identification of risks associated with adopting new technologies.

3. **SWOT Analysis**

   - **Definition**: Summarizing opportunities and threats in a SWOT matrix, along with internal strengths and weaknesses.

   - **Objectives**: Provide a comprehensive view of market dynamics and the company's internal capabilities.

   - **Advantages**: Helps develop strategies that leverage strengths and opportunities while mitigating weaknesses and threats.

4. **Contingency Plans**

   - **Definition**: Developing alternative plans to address major identified threats.

   - **Elements**: Identification of critical risks, mitigation strategies, emergency plans.

   - **Advantages**: Prepares the company to manage crisis situations and reduce the negative impact of threats.

Market analysis is a fundamental component of the business plan that provides an in-depth understanding of the industry, target customers, competitors, and opportunities and threats in the market. Accurate market research allows the collection of essential data for informed decision-making, while identifying the target customers helps develop marketing strategies and products that meet consumers' specific needs. Competitor analysis provides a clear view of the company's competitive positioning, enabling the identification of best practices and areas for improvement. Finally, evaluating market opportunities and threats allows the development of strategies that leverage emerging opportunities and mitigate risks, ensuring sustainable growth and a long-term competitive advantage.

# 4. Business Strategy in the Business Plan

The business strategy is the backbone of the business plan, as it defines the company's direction and objectives, how it intends to compete in the market, and how it plans to achieve its goals. A well-outlined business strategy helps clarify the company's vision and mission, establish measurable goals, and develop detailed marketing and sales plans. This section will explore the fundamental components of the business strategy: vision and mission, short- and long-term goals, business model, and marketing and sales strategies.

### Company Vision and Mission

#### Company Vision

The company vision represents the long-term aspiration of the company, defining the desired future and the impact the company intends to have on the world. It answers the question "Where do we want to go?" and serves as an inspiring guide for the team and stakeholders. A well-formulated vision is ambitious but realistic and reflects the company's core values.

**Example of Company Vision:**

"To become the global leader in providing innovative technological solutions that improve the quality of life."

#### Company Mission

The company mission describes the purpose and current activities of the company, answering the question "What do we do and why do we do it?" It clearly communicates the value the company offers to customers and how it intends to achieve its goals. A well-defined mission is concise, clear, and customer-oriented.

**Example of Company Mission:**

"To provide cutting-edge technological solutions that enhance our customers' efficiency and productivity through continuous innovation and excellent customer service."

### Short- and Long-Term Goals

Business goals provide clear direction and measure progress towards achieving the vision and mission. Goals can be divided into short-term (1-2 years) and long-term (3-5 years or more).

#### Short-Term Goals

Short-term goals are specific, measurable milestones that the company intends to achieve in the near future. They are often linked to concrete projects and include detailed actions to improve operations, launch new products, or expand the customer base.

**Examples of Short-Term Goals:**

- Increase sales by 20% within the next year.

- Launch a new product within six months.

- Improve customer satisfaction by 15% through the implementation of a new support system.

#### Long-Term Goals

Long-term goals reflect the company's strategic aspirations over an extended timeframe. They aim to position the company for sustainable, long-term growth.

**Examples of Long-Term Goals:**

- Become the market leader in the industry within the next five years.

- Expand international presence in at least ten new markets over the next five years.

- Achieve an annual growth rate of 15% over the next five years through continuous innovation and product line expansion.

### Business Model

The business model describes how the company creates, delivers, and captures value. It provides a clear structure of the company's operations, revenue sources, and costs. A well-defined business model helps understand the internal workings of the company and its unique value proposition.

#### Components of the Business Model

1. **Value Proposition**

   - **Description**: The value proposition identifies the unique benefits the company offers to its customers. It answers the question "Why should customers choose our products or services?"

   - **Example**: "We offer customized software solutions that reduce processing times by 50%, significantly improving our customers' operational efficiency."


2. **Customer Segments**

   - **Description**: Identification of the different customer groups the company intends to serve.

   - **Example**: "Small and medium-sized enterprises in the manufacturing sector seeking process automation solutions."


3. **Distribution Channels**

   - **Description**: The methods the company uses to reach and deliver its products or services to customers.

- **Example**: "Direct sales through our website and a network of authorized distributors."

4. **Customer Relationships**

   - **Description**: The ways in which the company interacts with customers to maintain and enhance relationships.

   - **Example**: "24/7 customer support, loyalty programs, and regular product updates."

5. **Revenue Streams**

   - **Description**: Identification of the various sources of the company's income.

   - **Example**: "Software sales, annual subscriptions for updates and maintenance, and customized consulting services."

6. **Key Resources**

   - **Description**: The resources needed to

create and deliver the value proposition.

   - **Example**: "Skilled technical staff, advanced technological infrastructure, and a network of strategic partners."

7. **Key Activities**

   - **Description**: The essential activities for the company's operation and success.

   - **Example**: "Software development, research and development, and marketing."

8. **Key Partnerships**

   - **Description**: The alliances and collaborations that help the company achieve its goals.

   - **Example**: "Partnerships with hardware suppliers and collaborations with universities for advanced research."

9. **Cost Structure**

   - **Description**: The main operating and

investment costs of the company.

   - **Example**: "Development costs, staff salaries, and marketing expenses."

### Marketing and Sales Strategies

Marketing and sales strategies are crucial for a company's success. They outline how the company intends to promote its products or services, attract and retain customers, and increase sales. These strategies must align with the company's vision and mission and support the achievement of short- and long-term goals.

#### Marketing Strategy

The marketing strategy defines the plan for reaching and communicating with the target customer base. It includes several key components:

1. **Market Analysis**

   - **Description**: Assessment of the target market, identification of trends and opportunities.

   - **Example**: "The market for automation software is rapidly growing, with increasing demand from SMEs seeking efficient solutions."


2. **Market Segmentation**

   - **Description**: Division of the market into distinct segments to better target marketing activities.

   - **Example**: "Market segments based on company size (small, medium, large enterprises) and industry sectors (manufacturing, services, etc.)."


3. **Positioning**

   - **Description**: Defining how the product or service will be perceived compared to competitors.

- **Example**: "Positioning our software as the most customizable and user-friendly solution in the SME market."

4. **Marketing Mix (4Ps)**

   - **Product**: Defining the features, benefits, and uniqueness of the product.

   - **Price**: Pricing strategy, including discounts and promotions.

   - **Promotion**: Promotional activities to raise awareness and stimulate interest.

   - **Place (Distribution)**: Channels through which products will be sold and distributed.

**Example of Marketing Mix:**

- **Product**: Customizable automation software.

- **Price**: Competitive pricing with monthly and annual subscription options.

- **Promotion**: Digital marketing campaigns, participation in industry fairs, and educational webinars.

- **Place**: Online sales through the company website and via an authorized distributor network.

#### Sales Strategy

The sales strategy describes the plan to convert potential customers into actual customers. It includes several key steps:

1. **Sales Process**

   - **Description**: Definition of the stages of the sales process, from initial contact to closing the sale.

   - **Example**: "Our sales process includes lead generation, lead qualification, product presentation, objection handling, and closing the sale."

2. **Sales Techniques**

   - **Description**: Techniques used to persuade customers and close sales.

   - **Example**: "Using live demonstrations, offering free trials, and tailoring presentations to address specific customer needs."


3. **Sales Force Training**

   - **Description**: Training programs to ensure the sales team is well-prepared and up-to-date.

   - **Example**: "Ongoing product training, advanced sales techniques, and communication skills development."


4. **Customer Relationship Management (CRM)**

   - **Description**: Use of CRM systems to monitor and manage customer interactions.

   - **Example**: "Implementing a CRM system to track customer interactions, manage sales opportunities, and improve post-sales service."

5. **Sales Goals**

   - **Description**: Definition of clear and measurable sales goals.

   - **Example**: "Quarterly sales targets for each sales team member, with performance-based incentives."

The business strategy is an essential component of the business plan that guides the company towards long-term success. It includes defining a clear vision and mission, establishing short- and long-term goals, outlining an effective business model, and developing targeted marketing and sales strategies. A well-articulated business strategy provides a clear roadmap to achieve desired milestones, keeping the company focused and competitive in the market.

# 5. Operational Plan in the Business Plan

The operational plan is a vital component of the business plan, outlining how the company intends to achieve its goals through the implementation of effective processes and efficient resource management. This section delves into the organizational structure, operational processes and workflows, location and infrastructure, and the necessary technology and tools.

### Organizational Structure

The organizational structure defines how the company is organized, detailing the roles and responsibilities of each team member. A well-defined structure ensures that all business activities are covered and responsibilities are clearly assigned.

#### Types of Organizational Structure

1. **Functional Structure**

   - **Description**: The company is divided into departments based on specific functions, such as marketing, sales, finance, production, and human resources.

   - **Advantages**: Specialization and expertise in various functions, clarity of roles.

   - **Disadvantages**: Possible communication issues between different departments, risk of silos.


2. **Matrix Structure**

   - **Description**: Combines the functional structure with project-based teams. Employees have dual membership: both in their functional department and in project teams.

   - **Advantages**: Flexibility, improved communication and collaboration across functions.

   - **Disadvantages**: Complexity in management, risk of conflicts of interest.

3. **Divisional Structure**

- **Description**: The company is divided into autonomous divisions, each responsible for a product line or geographic area.

- **Advantages**: Flexibility and adaptability to specific market needs, autonomy of divisions.

- **Disadvantages**: Possible duplication of resources, internal competition.

#### Example of Organizational Structure

**Diagram of a Functional Structure:**

- **CEO**
  - **Marketing Department**
    - Marketing Manager
    - Marketing Specialists
  - **Sales Department**
    - Sales Manager
    - Sales Representatives

- **Finance Department**

    - CFO

    - Accountants

  - **Production Department**

    - Production Manager

    - Production Workers

  - **Human Resources Department**

    - HR Manager

    - HR Specialists

#### Roles and Responsibilities Description

**CEO (Chief Executive Officer)**

- **Responsibilities**: Strategic vision, high-level decisions, investor relations.

- **Tasks**: Establish business objectives, manage top management, represent the company externally.

**Marketing Manager**

- **Responsibilities**: Planning and executing marketing strategies.

- **Tasks**: Manage advertising campaigns, analyze the market, coordinate marketing activities.


**Sales Manager**

- **Responsibilities**: Increasing sales, managing the sales team.

- **Tasks**: Define sales targets, train the team, monitor sales performance.


**CFO (Chief Financial Officer)**

- **Responsibilities**: Managing company finances, financial planning.

- **Tasks**: Prepare budgets and financial reports, monitor cash flows, manage banking and investor relations.


**Production Manager**

- **Responsibilities**: Overseeing production operations, optimizing processes.

- **Tasks**: Manage the supply chain, improve production efficiency, ensure product quality.

**HR Manager**

- **Responsibilities**: Managing personnel, developing human resources.

- **Tasks**: Recruitment, training, performance management, employee welfare.

### Operational Processes and Workflows

Operational processes and workflows are fundamental to ensuring that the company operates efficiently and productively. Clearly defining these processes helps optimize resources, reduce waste, and improve the quality of the product or service offered.

#### Definition of Operational Processes

1. **Production Process**

   - **Description**: The stages involved in creating the product.

   - **Steps**: Procuring raw materials, production, quality control, packaging, shipping.

   - **Objectives**: Efficiency, quality, delivery times.

2. **Sales Process**

   - **Description**: The activities necessary to sell the product or service.

   - **Steps**: Lead generation, lead qualification, product presentation, negotiation, closing the sale, post-sale.

   - **Objectives**: Increase sales, customer satisfaction.

3. **Marketing Process**

- **Description**: Activities to promote and publicize the product or service.

   - **Steps**: Market analysis, development of marketing strategies, implementation of campaigns, monitoring results.

   - **Objectives**: Increase brand awareness, lead generation, customer retention.

4. **Human Resources Management Process**

   - **Description**: Activities to manage personnel.

   - **Steps**: Recruitment, training, performance evaluation, benefits management.

   - **Objectives**: Ensure the company has the necessary skills, improve employee satisfaction.

#### Workflows

Workflows describe the path a task or process follows within the company, outlining who is responsible for each phase and how activities are interconnected.

**Example of Workflow for the Production Process:**

1. **Procurement of Raw Materials**

    - **Responsible**: Purchasing Department

    - **Activities**: Supplier selection, price negotiation, ordering raw materials.

2. **Production**

    - **Responsible**: Production Department

    - **Activities**: Transforming raw materials into finished products, monitoring production.

3. **Quality Control**

- **Responsible**: Quality Department

   - **Activities**: Inspecting finished products, verifying compliance with quality standards.

4. **Packaging**

   - **Responsible**: Logistics Department

   - **Activities**: Packaging finished products, preparing for shipment.

5. **Shipping**

   - **Responsible**: Logistics Department

   - **Activities**: Organizing shipments, managing delivery logistics.

### Location and Infrastructure

Location and infrastructure are critical components of the operational plan. They determine the efficiency of business operations and the ability to respond quickly to market needs.

#### Choosing the Location

1. **Proximity to Markets**

    - **Description**: Closeness to key target markets.

    - **Advantages**: Reduced transportation costs, improved delivery times.

2. **Accessibility**

    - **Description**: Ease of access for employees, suppliers, and customers.

    - **Advantages**: Greater convenience, talent attraction, facilitation of logistical operations.

3. **Operational Costs**

    - **Description**: Assessment of rental

costs, labor, and other operating expenses.

   - **Advantages**: Cost optimization, improved profitability.


4. **Available Infrastructure**

   - **Description**: Availability of adequate infrastructure, such as transportation, utilities, and communication services.

   - **Advantages**: Ensuring operational continuity, reducing the risk of interruptions.


#### Business Infrastructure


1. **Buildings and Facilities**

   - **Description**: Physical structures needed for business operations.

   - **Elements**: Offices, production plants, warehouses, distribution centers.

2. **Equipment and Machinery**

   - **Description**: Tools and machines used

for production and other business operations.

   - **Elements**: Production machines, packaging equipment, inventory management systems.

3. **Transportation Systems**

   - **Description**: Means of transport needed for logistics and distribution.

   - **Elements**: Company vehicles, contracts with carriers, logistics management systems.

4. **Communication Systems**

   - **Description**: Communication infrastructure needed for business operations.

   - **Elements**: Telephone systems, internet network, internal communication platforms.

### Technology and Necessary Tools

Technology and tools used by the company are essential for improving operational efficiency, ensuring product quality, and facilitating communication and information management.

#### Necessary Technology

1. **Enterprise Resource Planning (ERP) Software**

   - **Description**: Integrated software that supports the management of all business activities.

   - **Advantages**: Centralization of information, improved planning and control of operations.

2. **Customer Relationship Management (CRM) Software**

   - **Description**: Tools to manage customer relationships and track interactions.

   - **Advantages**: Improved customer

management, increased customer satisfaction.

3. **Production Automation Systems**

   - **Description**: Technologies to automate production processes.

   - **Advantages**: Increased efficiency, reduced errors, improved product quality.

4. **IT Security Systems**

   - **Description**: Technologies to protect business data and IT infrastructure.

   - **Advantages**: Protection against cyber threats, ensuring operational continuity.

#### Necessary Tools

1. **Internal Communication Tools**

   - **Description**: Platforms to facilitate communication among employees.

   - **Elements**: Company email, instant

messaging software, video conferencing platforms.

2. **Project Management Tools**

   - **Description**: Tools to plan, execute, and monitor business projects.

   - **Elements**: Project management software like Asana, Trello, or Microsoft Project.

3. **Data Analysis Tools**

   - **Description**: Tools to analyze business data and support decision-making.

   - **Elements**: Analytics software like Tableau, Power BI, or Google Analytics.

4. **Accounting and Finance Tools**

   - **Description**: Software to manage business accounting and finances.

   - **Elements**: Software like QuickBooks, SAP, or Oracle Financials.

The operational plan is a crucial component of the business plan that details how the company intends to achieve its operational goals. It includes the organizational structure, operational processes and workflows, location and infrastructure, and the necessary technology and tools. A well-defined operational plan ensures that the company operates efficiently, productively, and in alignment with strategic goals.

# 6. Financial Plan in the Business Plan

The financial plan is a crucial section of the business plan that outlines how the company intends to manage its financial resources to achieve its business objectives. This document includes financial forecasts, budgeting and cost management, break-even analysis, and guidelines on financing and investments. Accurate financial planning is essential for attracting investors, securing funding, and ensuring the long-term sustainability of the company.

### Financial Forecasts

Financial forecasts are estimates of the company's future financial performance. These include the projected income statement, balance sheet, and cash flow.

#### Projected Income Statement

The projected income statement, or profit and loss statement, shows expected revenues, costs, and profits for a future period.

- **Revenues**: Sales estimates based on market research, sales history, and growth projections.

- **Cost of Goods Sold (COGS)**: Estimates of direct costs associated with producing goods sold.

- **Gross Margin**: Difference between revenues and COGS.

- **Operating Expenses**: Indirect costs such as salaries, rent, marketing, and administrative expenses.

- **Operating Profit**: Gross margin minus operating expenses.

- **Net Profit**: Operating profit minus taxes and interest.

#### Projected Balance Sheet

The projected balance sheet shows the company's financial position at a future point in time.

- **Assets**: Resources controlled by the company, such as cash, receivables, inventory, and fixed assets.

- **Liabilities**: Company obligations, including short-term and long-term debts.

- **Equity**: Difference between assets and liabilities, representing the net value of the company.

#### Projected Cash Flow

The projected cash flow shows how changes in revenues and expenses will affect the company's liquidity.

- **Operating Cash Inflows**: Cash flows from the company's primary activities.

- **Operating Cash Outflows**: Payments for operating costs such as salaries, suppliers, and rent.

- **Cash Flows from Investing**: Expenditures on capital assets and other investments.

- **Cash Flows from Financing**: Inflows or outflows from financing activities such as loans or equity issuance.

- **Net Cash Flow**: Sum of operating, investing, and financing cash flows.

### Budgeting and Cost Management

Budgeting and cost management are essential for controlling expenses and maintaining profitability.

#### Budget Creation

1. **Sales Budget**

- **Description**: Revenue estimate based on sales forecasts.

- **Components**: Units sold, selling prices, growth forecasts.

2. **Production Budget**

    - **Description**: Estimate of costs associated with production.

    - **Components**: COGS, material costs, labor costs, manufacturing overhead.

3. **Operating Budget**

    - **Description**: Estimate of operating expenses.

    - **Components**: Salaries, marketing, administrative expenses, rent, utilities.

4. **Cash Flow Budget**

    - **Description**: Projection of cash inflows and outflows.

- **Components**: Operating cash inflows, operating cash outflows, capital expenditures, financing cash flows.

#### Cost Control

1. **Continuous Monitoring**

    - **Description**: Regularly track expenses against the budget.

    - **Tools**: Financial management software, monthly reports.

2. **Cost Reduction**

    - **Description**: Implement strategies to reduce expenses without compromising quality.

    - **Strategies**: Process automation, supplier negotiation, waste reduction.

3. **Variance Analysis**

- **Description**: Compare actual costs with budgeted costs to identify discrepancies.

   - **Tools**: Variance reports, root cause analysis.

### Break-Even Analysis

Break-even analysis determines the sales level needed to cover all business costs.

#### Break-Even Calculation

1. **Fixed Costs**

   - **Description**: Costs that do not vary with production levels.

   - **Examples**: Rent, administrative salaries, depreciation.

2. **Variable Costs**

   - **Description**: Costs that vary directly

with production levels.

   - **Examples**: Raw materials, direct labor, shipping costs.

3. **Unit Revenues**

   - **Description**: Selling price per unit of product.

4. **Unit Contribution Margin**

   - **Description**: Difference between unit revenues and unit variable costs.

   - **Formula**: Unit Contribution Margin = Unit Revenues - Unit Variable Costs.

5. **Break-Even Point in Units**

   - **Formula**: Break-Even Point (Units) = Fixed Costs / Unit Contribution Margin.

6. **Break-Even Point in Value**

   - **Formula**: Break-Even Point (Value) =

Break-Even Point (Units) * Unit Revenues.

#### Interpreting Results

- **Utility**: Determine the sales volume needed to cover costs and start generating profit.

- **Applications**: Production planning, pricing decisions, economic feasibility assessment.

### Financing and Investment Guidelines

This section describes how the company plans to finance its operations and invest for future growth.

#### Financing Sources

1. **Internal Financing**

- **Description**: Use of financial resources generated internally by the company.

- **Examples**: Reinvested profits, company reserves.

2. **External Financing**

   - **Description**: Obtaining financial resources from external sources.

   - **Examples**: Bank loans, bond issuances, equity issuance.

3. **Venture Capital and Private Equity Investments**

   - **Description**: Financing from institutional investors in exchange for equity stakes.

   - **Advantages**: Access to significant capital, strategic support.

   - **Disadvantages**: Ownership dilution, potential management interference.

4. **Public Financing and Incentives**

   - **Description**: Grants, subsidized loans, and tax incentives from government entities.

   - **Advantages**: Favorable conditions, developmental support.

   - **Disadvantages**: Bureaucracy, time to obtain.

#### Investment Planning

1. **Identifying Investment Opportunities**

   - **Description**: Evaluate investment opportunities that can generate growth and profitability.

   - **Examples**: Capacity expansion, new product development, strategic acquisitions.

2. **Investment Evaluation**

   - **Description**: Analyze the feasibility

and profitability of investments.

  - **Tools**: Net Present Value (NPV), Internal Rate of Return (IRR), payback period.


3. **Capital Planning**

  - **Description**: Allocate financial resources to support planned investments.

  - **Tools**: Investment budgeting, cash flow management, debt planning.


4. **Investment Monitoring**

  - **Description**: Monitor investment performance to ensure objectives are met.

  - **Tools**: Periodic reports, variance analysis, strategy reviews.


The financial plan is a fundamental part of the business plan that outlines how the company will manage its financial resources to achieve its goals. It includes detailed financial forecasts, budgeting and cost management, break-even analysis, and guidelines on financing and investments. A well-developed financial plan not only helps the company plan and manage its finances effectively but is also crucial for attracting investors and securing funding.

# 7. Risks and Mitigation in the Business Plan

Risk management is a crucial component of the business plan, as every business is subject to a variety of risks that can impact its success. Identifying and managing these risks proactively is essential to ensure the stability and growth of the company. This section explores in detail the identification of business risks, risk management strategies, and emergency planning.

### Identification of Business Risks

Identifying risks is the first step in risk management. It involves recognizing and documenting potential risks that could negatively impact the company.

#### Types of Business Risks

1. **Financial Risks**

- **Description**: Risks associated with managing the company's financial resources.

   - **Examples**: Interest rate fluctuations, customer insolvency, currency exchange rate changes.

2. **Operational Risks**

   - **Description**: Risks arising from the company's day-to-day operations.

   - **Examples**: Supply chain disruptions, equipment failures, production inefficiencies.

3. **Market Risks**

   - **Description**: Risks related to the market conditions in which the company operates.

   - **Examples**: Competition, changes in consumer demand, fluctuations in raw material prices.

4. **Reputational Risks**

   - **Description**: Risks that could damage

the company's image and reputation.

   - **Examples**: Negative reviews, corporate scandals, failures in customer service.


5. **Legal and Regulatory Risks**

   - **Description**: Risks arising from legal and regulatory issues.

   - **Examples**: Legal disputes, regulatory changes, legal violations.


6. **Environmental Risks**

   - **Description**: Risks related to natural events or environmental issues.

   - **Examples**: Natural disasters, pollution, climate change.


7. **Technological Risks**

   - **Description**: Risks associated with the technology used by the company.

- **Examples**: Cyber-attacks, technological obsolescence, IT system malfunctions.

#### Methods for Identifying Risks

1. **Brainstorming**

   - **Description**: Group sessions to generate a list of potential risks.

   - **Advantages**: Involves various viewpoints, promotes creativity.

2. **SWOT Analysis**

   - **Description**: Assessment of strengths, weaknesses, opportunities, and threats.

   - **Advantages**: Identifies risks in a strategic context.

3. **Interviews and Questionnaires**

   - **Description**: Gathering information from employees, suppliers, customers, and other stakeholders.

- **Advantages**: Deepens understanding of specific risks.

4. **Historical Data Analysis**

   - **Description**: Examining the company's historical data to identify past risks.

   - **Advantages**: Based on real experiences, provides concrete data.

5. **Benchmarking**

   - **Description**: Comparing with other companies in the industry to identify common risks.

   - **Advantages**: Provides an external perspective, highlights best practices.

### Risk Management Strategies

Once risks are identified, strategies must be developed to manage them. These strategies may include avoidance, reduction, transfer, or acceptance of the risk.

#### Risk Avoidance

- **Description**: Modifying business plans to eliminate the risk.

- **Examples**: Avoid entering unstable markets, steer clear of investing in unproven technologies.

#### Risk Reduction

- **Description**: Implementing measures to reduce the likelihood or impact of the risk.

- **Examples**: Implementing data backup systems, diversifying suppliers to avoid supply chain disruptions.

#### Risk Transfer

- **Description**: Transferring the risk to third parties through contracts or insurance.

- **Examples**: Business insurance, outsourcing contracts with liability clauses.

#### Risk Acceptance

- **Description**: Accepting the risk and preparing to manage its consequences.

- **Examples**: Creating financial reserves to cover potential losses, developing contingency plans.

### Emergency Plan

An emergency plan outlines the actions to take in case of emergencies or business crises. It is essential for ensuring operational continuity and minimizing the impact of crises.

#### Components of an Emergency Plan

1. **Identification of Potential Crises**

   - **Description**: Listing possible emergencies that the company might face.

   - **Examples**: Fires, floods, cyber-attacks, supply chain disruptions.

2. **Emergency Response Procedures**

   - **Description**: Detailing immediate actions to take in response to each emergency.

   - **Examples**: Building evacuation in case of fire, activation of backup systems in case of IT failures.

3. **Business Continuity Plans**

   - **Description**: Describing how to maintain business operations during and after the emergency.

   - **Examples**: Using alternate locations, remote work for employees, alternative supply contracts.

4. **Roles and Responsibilities**

   - **Description**: Assigning specific responsibilities to employees or teams for managing emergencies.

   - **Examples**: Creating a crisis team, designating a company spokesperson, assigning coordination roles.


5. **Crisis Communication**

   - **Description**: Establishing protocols for communicating with employees, customers, suppliers, and media during a crisis.

   - **Examples**: Internal communication guidelines, press releases, media relations management.


6. **Training and Drills**

   - **Description**: Planning exercises and training sessions to prepare staff for emergencies.

   - **Examples**: Evacuation drills, security

protocol training, data recovery exercises.

### Case Study: Risk Management in a Manufacturing Company

#### Scenario

A medium-sized manufacturing company operates in a highly competitive sector. The company faces various risks including supply chain disruptions, fluctuations in raw material prices, and cyber-attacks.

#### Risk Identification

1. **Supply Chain Disruptions**

    - **Risk**: Delays in the delivery of raw materials can slow down production.

    - **Strategy**: Diversify suppliers, maintain safety stock, implement contracts with penalty clauses for delays.

2. **Fluctuations in Raw Material Prices**

   - **Risk**: Sudden price increases can reduce profit margins.

   - **Strategy**: Use long-term contracts to stabilize prices, implement just-in-time purchasing practices.

3. **Cyber Attacks**

   - **Risk**: Cyber-attacks can compromise sensitive data and disrupt operations.

   - **Strategy**: Implement advanced cybersecurity systems, train staff on IT security, create incident response plans.

#### Implementation of Risk Management Strategies

1. **Supplier Diversification**

   - **Actions**: Identify and qualify alternative suppliers, negotiate favorable contracts, establish strong relationships with critical suppliers.

   - **Tools**: Develop a supplier database, use risk management software to track supplier performance.

2. **Stock Management**

   - **Actions**: Activate accumulated safety stock to maintain ongoing production until normal supply is restored, helping to avoid significant production interruptions.

   - **Tools**: Implement an inventory management system with accurate demand forecasts to optimize safety stock.

3. **Communication and Coordination**

   - **Actions**: Establish a crisis team to manage supply chain disruption and coordinate actions between departments. Timely and clear communications with customers and suppliers are crucial to maintaining trust and managing expectations.

   - **Tools**: Use corporate communication tools such as email, instant messaging systems, and collaboration platforms to keep everyone informed.

4. **Post-Event Analysis**

   - **Actions**: After managing the disruption, conduct a detailed assessment to identify the causes of the disruption and evaluate the effectiveness of the responses adopted. This helps improve future emergency plans and prevent similar incidents.

   - **Tools**: Draft a post-incident report and update the emergency plan based on lessons learned.

#### Raw Material Price Increases

1. **Review of Sales Prices**

   - **Actions**: Analyze the impact of raw material price increases on production costs and profit margins. Based on this analysis, decide whether and how to increase product sales prices to maintain profitability.

- **Tools**: Use financial analysis software to evaluate the effects of price increases on profits and costs.

2. **Search for Alternatives**

   - **Actions**: Explore alternative materials or sourcing options that can reduce the impact of price increases. This may involve searching for new suppliers or adopting cheaper materials.

   - **Tools**: Conduct comparative analyses of suppliers and materials through market research reports and feasibility studies.

3. **Negotiation with Suppliers**

   - **Actions**: Negotiate with existing suppliers to obtain better terms or lock in raw material prices for extended periods. This strategy can help stabilize costs and prevent sudden fluctuations.

   - **Tools**: Use long-term contracts and purchase agreements that include price review clauses.

4. **Financial Planning**

   - **Actions**: Update budgets and financial forecasts to reflect increased raw material costs. Anticipate higher expenses and plan how to address potential impacts on cash flow and profitability.

   - **Tools**: Adapt the financial plan and use cost planning and analysis tools.

#### Cyber Attack

1. **Activation of Incident Response Plan**

   - **Actions**: Immediately after a cyber-attack, it is crucial to activate the incident response plan, which should include blocking the attack, isolating compromised systems, and notifying the relevant authorities.

   - **Tools**: Use cybersecurity tools to monitor and contain the attack, such as firewalls and intrusion detection software.

2. **Notification and Communication**

- **Actions**: Promptly communicate with all stakeholders, including customers and business partners, about the incident and the measures taken to mitigate the damage. It is important to maintain transparency and provide regular updates.

   - **Tools**: Draft press releases and use corporate communication platforms to inform stakeholders.

3. **Recovery and Restoration**

   - **Actions**: Perform data and system recovery using recent backups. Verify that all systems are secure and functioning properly before resuming normal operations.

   - **Tools**: Use data backup and recovery tools to restore information and systems.

4. **Security Analysis and Improvement**

   - **Actions**: After managing the incident, conduct a detailed analysis to understand how the attack occurred and what security measures can be improved. Update security policies and procedures to prevent future attacks.

- **Tools**: Perform security audits and implement new protection measures, such as software updates and ongoing staff training.

Effective risk management and emergency planning are essential for ensuring business resilience and operational continuity. Identifying business risks, developing management strategies, and having a well-defined emergency plan allow companies to effectively handle crises and minimize negative impacts on operations and reputation. Through a structured and proactive approach to risk management, businesses can improve their recovery capability and continue to thrive even in adverse situations.

# 8. Drafting the Business Plan

Drafting a business plan is a fundamental process for planning and managing any entrepreneurial venture. A well-written business plan not only guides the company in achieving its goals but also serves as a communication tool with potential investors, partners, and other stakeholders. This section explores the essential steps for compiling the various chapters of the business plan, the importance of style and language, and the need for clarity and conciseness.

### Compiling the Various Chapters

A business plan consists of several chapters, each addressing specific aspects of the business and its project. Each chapter should be compiled with attention to detail and provide complete and accurate information. Here is an overview of the main chapters and what to include in each:

#### 1. **Executive Summary**

- **Description**: This chapter provides a concise and engaging overview of the entire business plan. It should grab the reader's attention and encourage them to continue reading.

- **Contents**: Summary of the company's mission, the products or services offered, the target market, key objectives, and financial projections. It should include a brief description of the business model and the main competitive advantages.

- **Tips**: Although it is the first section of the plan, it is often easier to write the Executive Summary after completing the other chapters.

#### 2. **Company Description**

- **Description**: Provides details about the company, its history, legal structure, and organization.

- **Contents**: Information on the company's mission and vision, legal structure (limited liability company, joint-stock company, etc.), physical location, and an overview of the management team.

- **Tips**: Highlight the company's strengths and unique resources. Include major achievements and successes to date.

#### 3. **Market Analysis**

- **Description**: Analyzes the market in which the company operates or intends to enter.

- **Contents**: Market research, identification of the target customer base, competition analysis, and assessment of opportunities and threats. This chapter should demonstrate a thorough understanding of the industry and market dynamics.

- **Tips**: Use recent data and reliable sources to support your claims. Include charts and tables to illustrate market trends.

#### 4. **Business Strategy**

- **Description**: Describes the company's strategy for achieving its goals.

- **Contents**: Business vision and mission, short-term and long-term objectives, business model, and marketing and sales strategies. Detail how the company plans to position itself in the market and reach its target audience.

- **Tips**: Be specific and realistic about the strategies and expected outcomes. Show how the strategies align with the company's resources and capabilities.

#### 5. **Operational Plan**

- **Description**: Details the daily operations and resources needed to run the business.

- **Contents**: Organizational structure, operational processes and workflows, location and infrastructure, and necessary technology and tools. This chapter should provide a clear description of how the company performs its activities and manages its resources.

- **Tips**: Include process diagrams and organizational charts to clarify the organizational structure and workflows.

#### 6. **Financial Plan**

- **Description**: Presents financial projections and funding requirements.

- **Contents**: Financial projections (budget forecast, income statement, balance sheet), budgeting and cost management, break-even analysis, and indications of required funding and investments. It should demonstrate the financial viability of the project and its ability to generate returns.

- **Tips**: Use detailed financial models based on realistic assumptions. Include tables and charts to visually represent the projections.

#### 7. **Risks and Mitigation**

- **Description**: Identifies potential risks and strategies for mitigating them.

- **Contents**: Identification of business risks, risk management strategies, and emergency plan. It should show the company's preparedness to handle potential crises and ensure operational continuity.

- **Tips**: Be clear and detailed about specific risks and preventive actions. Regularly update the emergency plan based on changes in the business context and market.

### Style and Language of the Business Plan

The way a business plan is written is as crucial as the content itself. The style and language should be professional, clear, and suitable for the intended audience.

#### 1. **Professionalism**

- **Description**: The business plan should

reflect a high level of professionalism. Use formal and technical language, avoiding colloquial or informal expressions.

- **Tips**: Ensure the document is well-structured and consistently formatted. Use a serious and objective tone, and ensure that all information is presented professionally.

#### 2. **Clarity**

- **Description**: Clarity is essential to ensure that the information is easily understandable and accessible.

- **Tips**: Use concise sentences and avoid unnecessary technical jargon. Explain complex concepts simply and directly. Use headings and subheadings to organize information and make the document more readable.

#### 3. **Consistency**

- **Description**: The business plan must be consistent in terms of content and style.

- **Tips**: Ensure that information presented in different chapters is aligned and not contradictory. Use a uniform writing style and maintain consistent terminology.

#### 4. **Accuracy**

- **Description**: The information must be accurate and based on concrete data.

- **Tips**: Verify the data and sources cited. Avoid making unsupported claims or overstating projections.

### Importance of Clarity and Conciseness

Clarity and conciseness are fundamental to ensuring that the business plan is effective and comprehensible. A well-written document facilitates understanding and increases the likelihood of success in communicating with investors and other stakeholders.

#### 1. **Clarity**

- **Description**: Clarity helps readers easily understand the information and make informed decisions.

- **Tips**: Avoid ambiguity and provide detailed explanations where necessary. Use graphs and tables to visually represent complex data and facilitate understanding.

#### 2. **Conciseness**

- **Description**: Being concise means presenting information directly and without superfluity.

- **Tips**: Eliminate non-essential details and maintain focus on the key aspects of the business plan. Each section should be well-structured and focused on specific objectives.

Drafting a business plan requires attention to detail and thorough preparation. Compiling each chapter with precision, using a professional style and language, and ensuring clarity and conciseness are key elements for creating an effective and persuasive document. A well-written business plan not only guides the company in achieving its goals but also serves as a powerful communication tool with investors and partners, increasing the chances of success and growth in the market.

# 9. Presenting the Business Plan

Presenting a business plan is a crucial moment that can determine success in securing funding, attracting partners, or simply validating the entrepreneurial idea. An effective presentation must not only clearly communicate the project's value but also demonstrate preparedness and management capability. This section explores presentation techniques, preparation for investor meetings, and how to respond to questions and objections effectively.

### Presentation Techniques

The presentation of a business plan should be well-planned and structured. Using appropriate techniques helps maintain the audience's attention and convey information effectively.

#### 1. **Preparation and Planning**

- **Structuring the Presentation**: Organize the presentation in a logical and coherent manner, following the order of the business plan chapters. Start with an engaging introduction, followed by an overview of the company, market analysis, strategy, operational plan, and financial plan, and conclude with risk management and conclusions.

- **Duration**: Limit the presentation to 20-30 minutes, allowing time for questions and answers. Avoid overwhelming the audience with too much information in a short period.

#### 2. **Using Visual Aids**

- **Slides and Charts**: Use visual aids such as slides and charts to represent key data and information. Ensure that slides are clear, well-designed, and free of excessive text. Charts should be easily readable and relevant to the points being discussed.

- **Videos and Demos**: Consider using short videos or demonstrations to illustrate the product or service in action. These tools can make the presentation more dynamic and engaging.

#### 3. **Presentation Style**

- **Clarity and Simplicity**: Speak clearly and simply, avoiding technical jargon and complicated terms. Use concrete examples and success stories to illustrate key points.

- **Enthusiasm and Passion**: Show enthusiasm and passion for the project. This can be contagious and help persuade the audience of the idea's validity and potential.

#### 4. **Audience Engagement**

- **Involvement**: Engage the audience with questions and solicit feedback. This not only keeps their attention high but can also provide valuable insights into how the business plan is perceived.

- **Adaptation**: Be prepared to adapt the presentation based on the audience's reactions and interests. If a particular topic sparks interest, delve deeper without straying too far from the plan.

### Preparing for Investor Meetings

Preparing for a meeting with investors is essential for presenting the business plan effectively and persuasively. Here are some key steps for adequate preparation:

#### 1. **Research on Investors**

- **Investor Profile**: Study potential investors to understand their interests, experience, and preferred sectors. This helps tailor the presentation and better address their needs and expectations.

- **Previous Investments**: Analyze the companies they have invested in previously. This can provide insights into what they are looking for and how to position your project more attractively.

#### 2. **Prepare Detailed Responses**

- **Frequently Asked Questions**: Prepare answers to common questions investors might ask. These usually cover market strategy, financial sustainability, the management team, and risks.

- **Evidence and Data**: Be ready to provide concrete data and evidence to support the claims made in the business plan. Investors value fact-based information over vague statements.

#### 3. **Simulate the Interview**

- **Practice Sessions**: Conduct practice sessions with colleagues or mentors to simulate the interview. This helps improve performance and prepares you to respond smoothly and confidently.

- **Feedback**: Request feedback on your responses and overall presentation. Use this information to make improvements.

#### 4. **Supporting Materials**

- **Documentation**: Have copies of the business plan and any other supporting materials (such as executive summaries, financial spreadsheets) available for distribution to investors. This demonstrates preparedness and professionalism.

- **Brochures and Fact Sheets**: Create brochures or fact sheets summarizing the key points of the presentation. These materials can be useful for investors for future reference.

### Responding to Questions and Objections

During an investor meeting, questions and objections are inevitable. Being able to respond effectively is crucial for maintaining interest and building trust.

#### 1. **Response Techniques**

- **Active Listening**: Listen carefully to questions and objections before responding. This shows respect and awareness of the investor's concerns.

- **Clear and Concise Answers**: Provide clear and concise answers. Avoid digressing and stay focused on the questions asked. Use concrete examples and data to support your responses.

- **Admitting Uncertainties**: If you don't have an immediate answer, it's better to admit uncertainty rather than provide inaccurate information. Commit to providing a complete response later, if necessary.

#### 2. **Handling Objections**

- **Welcoming Objections**: Show openness to objections and use them as opportunities to demonstrate preparedness and knowledge. Don't take objections personally; view them as useful feedback.

- **Highlighting Solutions**: For each objection, present a solution or mitigation strategy. Show how the company intends to address and overcome the identified challenges.

- **Staying Positive**: Maintain a positive and constructive attitude even when faced with difficult questions or criticism. This helps build trust and demonstrates the ability to handle difficulties.

#### 3. **Conclusion and Follow-Up**

- **Reaffirm Key Points**: At the end of the presentation and discussions, summarize the key points and emphasize the main advantages of the company and the project.

- **Commit to Follow-Up**: Offer to provide additional information or documentation if needed and establish a plan for follow-up. This demonstrates commitment and willingness to collaborate.

Presenting a business plan is a complex process that requires preparation, professionalism, and communication skills. Using effective presentation techniques, preparing adequately for investor meetings, and handling questions and objections well are crucial elements for success. A well-planned and structured approach not only improves the chances of securing funding or partnerships but also demonstrates the company's seriousness and preparedness. A well-executed presentation can make the difference between a project that takes off and one that remains on paper.

# 10. Monitoring and Revising the Business Plan

Monitoring and revising the business plan are essential to ensure that a company stays on the right track towards achieving its goals and adapts to market changes and new challenges. Keeping the plan updated and relevant allows businesses to optimize their operations, improve their strategy, and ensure sustainable growth. This section explores the importance of continuous monitoring, key performance indicators (KPIs), and practices for revising and adapting the business plan.

### Importance of Continuous Monitoring

Continuous monitoring of the business plan is crucial for several reasons:

#### 1. **Adapting to Market Changes**

- **Market Evolution**: Markets are dynamic and can change rapidly due to new trends, technological innovations, or shifts in consumer preferences. Continuous monitoring allows for the detection of these changes and the adjustment of the business strategy accordingly.

- **Responsiveness**: A company that regularly monitors market conditions can promptly respond to new opportunities and threats, optimizing its resources and strategies.

#### 2. **Measuring Results**

- **Business Performance**: Monitoring performance against the objectives set in the business plan helps assess whether the company is achieving the expected results. This helps identify areas of success and areas needing improvement.

- **Data-Driven Decisions**: Strategic decisions based on real-time, updated data are generally more accurate and informed compared to those based on initial forecasts or assumptions.

#### 3. **Risk Management**

- **Identifying Issues**: Continuous monitoring helps detect any issues or deviations from the initial plan, allowing for intervention before problems become severe.

- **Corrective Actions**: With a clear view of performance and issues, the company can implement corrective measures promptly to mitigate risks and maintain control over operations.

#### 4. **Continuous Improvement**

- **Process Optimization**: Regular monitoring provides feedback on which processes and strategies are most effective, allowing for improvements and optimization of business operations.

- **Innovation**: Monitoring performance

can also drive innovation, pushing the company to find more efficient and innovative ways to achieve its goals.

### Key Performance Indicators (KPIs)

Key Performance Indicators (KPIs) are metrics used to assess a company's success in achieving its objectives. These indicators vary depending on the type of business, specific goals, and areas of focus. Here are some main categories of KPIs that companies can monitor:

#### 1. **Financial KPIs**

- **Revenue and Profit**: Metrics such as revenue, gross and net profit margins, and return on investment (ROI) provide essential information about the company's financial health.

- **Cash Flow**: Monitoring operating, investing, and financing cash flows helps ensure the company has the resources needed for daily operations and growth.

- **Costs and Expenses**: Indicators such as customer acquisition cost (CAC) and cost per unit of production provide insights into how much the company is spending to achieve its goals.

#### 2. **Marketing and Sales KPIs**

- **Customer Acquisition**: Measuring the number of new customers acquired, lead conversion rates, and cost per lead can provide insights into the effectiveness of marketing strategies.

- **Customer Retention**: Metrics such as customer retention rate, customer lifetime value (CLV), and customer satisfaction (Net Promoter Score) help understand how well the company retains and satisfies its customers.

- **Sales Performance**: KPIs such as sales volume, average order value, and sales growth rate can provide a clear picture of the effectiveness of sales strategies.

#### 3. **Operational KPIs**

- **Operational Efficiency**: Measuring the efficiency of business processes through indicators such as production cycle time, error rates in production, and downtime can help optimize operations.

- **Service Quality**: Metrics like response time to customer inquiries, number of complaints, and issue resolution time can provide insights into the quality of service provided.

#### 4. **Human Resources KPIs**

- **Employee Satisfaction**: Measuring employee satisfaction and engagement through surveys and feedback can help maintain a positive and productive work environment.

- **Employee Turnover**: Monitoring employee turnover rates and reasons for departure can provide insights into improving retention and the effectiveness of human resource management.

### Revising and Adapting the Business Plan

The business plan should be a dynamic document, updated and adapted in response to internal and external changes. Periodic revision of the business plan is essential to keep it relevant and aligned with the business reality.

#### 1. **When to Revise the Business Plan**

- **Periodic Reviews**: Schedule regular reviews of the business plan, such as annually or semi-annually, to assess progress and make necessary adjustments.

- **Significant Events**: Conduct extraordinary revisions following significant events, such as market changes, new opportunities, business crises, or strategic modifications.

#### 2. **Revision Process**

- **Performance Assessment**: Analyze performance against KPIs and the objectives set in the business plan. Identify areas of positive results and those needing improvement.

- **Updating Projections**: Review and update financial projections and forecasts based on current data and recent performance. This includes budget forecasts, spending plans, and cash flow projections.

- **Strategy Modification**: Make adjustments to the business strategy based on new information and updated market conditions. This may involve changes in marketing strategy, operations, or risk management.

- **Feedback and Engagement**: Involve the management team and other stakeholders in the revision process to gather feedback and ensure the revised plan reflects a shared and realistic vision.

#### 3. **Implementing Changes**

- **Action Plan**: Develop a detailed action plan for implementing changes to the business plan. Define responsibilities, timelines, and resources needed for implementation.

- **Monitoring Changes**: Monitor the effectiveness of the implemented changes and ensure that new strategies and plans are adopted and followed correctly.

#### 4. **Communicating Revisions**

- **Updating Stakeholders**: Communicate changes to the business plan to investors, partners, and other relevant stakeholders. Provide a summary of the changes and the reasons for them.

- **Documentation**: Update the business

plan document and distribute revised versions to team members and stakeholders to ensure everyone is aligned with the updated plan.

Monitoring and revising the business plan are critical components for a company's long-term success. Continuous control through KPIs and regular reviews allows for adaptation to market dynamics, optimization of operations, and effective risk management. A dynamic and updated business plan not only improves resource and strategy management but also ensures sustainable growth and maximizes value for investors and other stakeholders. Investing time and resources in monitoring and revising the business plan is a practice that can significantly impact the company's success and resilience over time.

# 11. Practical Examples of Business Plans

Business plans are crucial tools for any enterprise, whether it's a startup in its launch phase or an established company in the process of expansion. Examining concrete examples of business plans can provide practical insights into structuring and drafting a detailed and effective plan. Below are three detailed examples of business plans for different types of businesses: a tech startup, a new coffee shop, and a consulting firm. Each example includes a comprehensive description of the various chapters and key elements.

### Example 1: Tech Startup

#### 1. **Introduction and Executive Summary**

- **Company Name**: TechInnovate

- **Description**: TechInnovate is a startup developing artificial intelligence solutions to enhance business productivity.

- **Objective**: Achieve a 10% market share in the SME tech sector by the third year.

- **Funding Request**: €1 million for product launch and marketing activities.

#### 2. **Market Analysis**

- **Market Research**: The demand for AI solutions in SMEs is growing by 25% annually. The sector is characterized by rapid technological development and increasing adoption of emerging technologies.

- **Target Customers**: Small and medium-sized enterprises in the manufacturing and service sectors looking to optimize processes and increase efficiency.

- **Competition Analysis**: Major competitors include AI Solutions and SmartTech. TechInnovate differentiates itself through its customizable platform and continuous support.

- **Opportunities and Threats**:

Opportunities include the growing adoption of AI in SMEs, while threats are rapid technological evolution and fierce competition.

#### 3. **Business Strategy**

- **Vision and Mission**: Vision to become a leader in AI solutions for SMEs. Mission to provide intelligent tools to improve business productivity and reduce costs.

- **Objectives**: Short-term goal of market launch with a pilot product; long-term goal of expanding the customer base and optimizing product features.

- **Business Model**: Sale of software licenses with a monthly or annual subscription model, with options for paid customization.

- **Marketing and Sales Strategies**: Digital marketing campaigns, participation in tech fairs, and collaborations with strategic partners in the IT sector.

#### 4. **Operational Plan**

- **Organizational Structure**: CEO, CTO, CMO, software developers, and customer support staff.

- **Operational Processes and Workflows**: Agile product development, continuous testing, and post-sales support.

- **Location and Infrastructure**: Main office in a major tech city, with cloud resources for hosting and development.

- **Technology and Tools**: Use of software development tools like GitHub and cloud computing platforms like AWS.

#### 5. **Financial Plan**

- **Financial Projections**: Revenue projection of €500,000 in the first year, increasing to €2 million by the third year. Expected profit margin of 20%.

- **Budgeting and Cost Management**:

Budget of €500,000 for development and marketing in the first year. Strict cost management through monthly monitoring.

- **Break-even Analysis**: Break-even point expected by the second year, with revenues sufficient to cover fixed and variable costs.

- **Funding and Investments**: Request for €1 million from venture capital investors to cover initial development and marketing costs.

#### 6. **Risk and Mitigation**

- **Risk Identification**: Risk of product development delays, rapid changes in AI technology, and market adoption issues.

- **Risk Management Strategies**: Contingency planning for delays, regular technology updates, and targeted marketing strategies to increase adoption.

- **Emergency Plan**: Creation of a plan for customer support in case of technical issues and resource planning to handle potential crises.

### Example 2: New Coffee Shop

#### 1. **Introduction and Executive Summary**

- **Company Name**: Café Delizioso
- **Description**: Café Delizioso is a new coffee shop located in the city center, offering high-quality coffee, artisanal baked goods, and a cozy atmosphere.
- **Objective**: Become the go-to spot for high-quality coffee in the area within the first year.
- **Funding Request**: €150,000 for startup and shop setup.

#### 2. **Market Analysis**

- **Market Research**: The specialty coffee market is growing by 10% annually. The demand for gourmet coffee and cozy environments is particularly high among professionals and city center residents.

- **Target Customers**: Professionals, university students, and local residents seeking a place to socialize and enjoy high-quality coffee.

- **Competition Analysis**: Major competitors include local coffee shops and international chains. Café Delizioso stands out for product quality and unique atmosphere.

- **Opportunities and Threats**: Opportunities include the growing demand for gourmet experiences, while threats include competition and variable supplier costs.

#### 3. **Business Strategy**

- **Vision and Mission**: Vision to become the reference coffee shop in the city for coffee quality and hospitality. Mission to offer a premium coffee experience in a welcoming and distinctive environment.

- **Objectives**: Short-term goal to break

even in the first year; long-term goal to expand the customer base and consider opening new locations.

- **Business Model**: Sale of coffee and baked goods with a premium pricing model, and subscription offers for regular customers.

- **Marketing and Sales Strategies**: Local advertising, social media campaigns, and collaborations with local businesses for events and promotions.

#### 4. **Operational Plan**

- **Organizational Structure**: Owner, store manager, baristas, and kitchen and service staff.

- **Operational Processes and Workflows**: Daily ingredient preparation, customer service, inventory management, and maintaining quality standards.

- **Location and Infrastructure**: Shop located in a high-traffic area of the city center, with high-quality furnishings and equipment.

- **Technology and Tools**: Use of professional coffee machines, POS systems for sales and inventory management, and digital marketing tools.

#### 5. **Financial Plan**

- **Financial Projections**: Revenue projection of €200,000 in the first year, increasing to €350,000 by the third year. Expected profit margin of 15%.

- **Budgeting and Cost Management**: Budget of €100,000 for initial setup and €50,000 for marketing and operations. Monthly cost and expense monitoring.

- **Break-even Analysis**: Break-even point expected in the first year, with sales sufficient to cover fixed and variable costs.

- **Funding and Investments**: Request for €150,000 to cover startup and initial marketing and furnishing expenses.

#### 6. **Risk and Mitigation**

- **Risk Identification**: Risks related to competition and fluctuations in raw material costs.

- **Risk Management Strategies**: Diversification of suppliers and customer loyalty strategies to maintain a solid base of regular customers.

- **Emergency Plan**: Creation of a plan to address periods of low traffic and maintaining a liquidity reserve to cover unforeseen events.

### Example 3: Consulting Firm

#### 1. **Introduction and Executive Summary**

- **Company Name**: ConsultPro

- **Description**: ConsultPro is a consulting firm specializing in business strategy and change management for medium-sized companies.

- **Objective**: Become one of the leading

providers of consulting services in the region by the second year.

- **Funding Request**: €250,000 for launch and initial growth.

#### 2. **Market Analysis**

- **Market Research**: The business consulting market is growing with increasing demand for experts in change management and business strategy optimization.

- **Target Customers**: Medium-sized businesses needing support to optimize their business strategies and manage organizational changes.

- **Competition Analysis**: Major competitors include large consulting firms and freelance consultants. ConsultPro differentiates itself through a personalized approach and specialization.

- **Opportunities and Threats**: Opportunities include the growing need for specialized consulting services, while threats include competition from major players and demand variability.

#### 3. **Business Strategy**

- **Vision and Mission**: Vision to become the main strategic partner for medium-sized businesses in the region. Mission to provide personalized consulting that guides companies towards sustainable growth and positive change.

- **Objectives**: Short-term goal to acquire 10 main clients in the first year; long-term goal to expand services and increase the client base.

- **Business Model**: Business model based on hourly rates and long-term projects with options for ongoing consulting.

- **Marketing and Sales Strategies**: Networking with other businesses and professionals, participating in events and conferences, and digital marketing focused on SEO and content.

#### 4. **Operational Plan**

- **Organizational Structure**: Founders, senior consultants, analysts, and administrative staff.

- **Operational Processes and Workflows**: Project management, development of strategic plans for clients, and performance monitoring.

- **Location and Infrastructure**: Main office in a central area, with online collaboration tools to facilitate remote work with clients.

- **Technology and Tools**: Use of project management software, data analysis tools, and communication and collaboration platforms.

#### 5. **Financial Plan**

- **Financial Projections**: Revenue projection of €300,000 in the first year, increasing to €600,000 by the third year. Expected profit margin of 25%.

- **Budgeting and Cost Management**: Budget of €150,000 for startup and marketing, and €100,000 for operating expenses. Continuous cost and expense monitoring.

- **Break-even Analysis**: Break-even point expected by the second year, with revenues sufficient to cover fixed and variable costs.

- **Funding and Investments**: Request for €250,000 to cover initial costs and finance marketing and operations activities.

#### 6. **Risk and Mitigation**

- **Risk Identification**: Risk of slower-than-expected client acquisition and fluctuations in the consulting market.

- **Risk Management Strategies**: Diversification of services offered and building a solid network of contacts to ensure a steady client flow.

- **Emergency Plan**: Planning measures to maintain liquidity and strategies to address potential declines in demand.

These examples of business plans illustrate how

companies can structure their plans to address specific challenges and capitalize on market opportunities. Each business plan must be tailored to the unique needs and circumstances of the company, but following a well-defined structure helps ensure that all fundamental aspects are considered and effectively addressed. A detailed and well-drafted business plan not only guides the company in its growth but also clearly communicates the value and vision to potential investors and stakeholders.

## 12. Glossary of Key Terms in Business Planning

Business planning is a field rich in technical and specific terminology. Understanding key terms is essential for effectively drafting, interpreting, and applying a business plan. This glossary provides a comprehensive overview of the most relevant terms in the context of business planning, explaining their meaning and importance.

#### 1. **Business Plan**

- **Definition**: A strategic document that outlines a company's goals, strategies for achieving them, required resources, and financial projections. It serves as a guide for managing the business and as a tool for attracting investors.

- **Importance**: Provides an overall vision of the business plan, facilitating planning and communication with stakeholders and potential investors.

#### 2. **Executive Summary**

- **Definition**: A concise summary of the business plan that includes key aspects of the project, such as the company vision, main objectives, and funding needs.

- **Importance**: Serves as an introduction to the plan, allowing readers to quickly get an overview of the key information and value proposition.


#### 3. **Market Analysis**

- **Definition**: The assessment of market dynamics, including market size, trends, and opportunities and threats. It includes market segmentation and competitive analysis.

- **Importance**: Provides an understanding of the context in which the company operates, helping to identify opportunities and formulate appropriate strategies.


#### 4. **Target Customer**

- **Definition**: The specific segment of customers that a company targets with its products or services. This can be defined by demographic, behavioral, or geographic characteristics.

- **Importance**: Identifying the target customer helps to focus marketing strategies and product offerings on the needs and preferences of the intended audience.

#### 5. **Competitive Analysis**

- **Definition**: The evaluation of direct and indirect competitors, including their strengths, weaknesses, strategies, and market positioning.

- **Importance**: Allows for identifying areas of differentiation and developing effective competitive strategies.

#### 6. **Opportunities and Threats**

- **Definition**: Opportunities represent potential areas of growth or market advantage, while threats are risks or challenges that could negatively impact the company.

- **Importance**: Helps to understand the

external environment and plan strategies to capitalize on opportunities and mitigate threats.

#### 7. **Company Vision**

- **Definition**: A statement describing the future direction of the company and what it aspires to become in the long term.

- **Importance**: Guides strategy and business decisions, providing a clear image of the desired future.

#### 8. **Company Mission**

- **Definition**: A statement that defines the company's reason for being and its main purpose. It explains why the company exists and what value it offers to customers.

- **Importance**: Defines the company's identity and guides daily activities and strategies.

#### 9. **Short-Term and Long-Term

Goals**

- **Definition**: Short-term goals are objectives to be achieved within a relatively short period (e.g., 1 year), while long-term goals extend over a longer period (e.g., 3-5 years).

- **Importance**: Setting clear goals helps in planning and monitoring progress toward the company vision.

#### 10. **Business Model**

- **Definition**: The structure through which a company creates, delivers, and captures value. It includes revenue sources, costs, and key resources.

- **Importance**: Defines how the company operates and generates revenue, influencing all strategic decisions.

#### 11. **Marketing and Sales Strategies**

- **Definition**: The plans and actions taken to promote and sell the company's products or services. Includes advertising, promotions, and sales techniques.

- **Importance**: Essential for attracting and retaining customers and achieving sales and growth objectives.

#### 12. **Organizational Structure**

- **Definition**: The arrangement and coordination of human resources and business functions. Includes roles and responsibilities of each team member.

- **Importance**: Determines how business activities are managed and facilitates operational efficiency.

#### 13. **Operational Processes and Workflows**

- **Definition**: The methods and procedures used to carry out the company's daily activities. Includes resource management and workflow optimization.

- **Importance**: Essential for ensuring that operations are conducted efficiently and that products or services are delivered according to standards.

#### 14. **Location and Infrastructure**

- **Definition**: The physical location of the company and the resources needed for its operations, including offices, warehouses, and equipment.

- **Importance**: Affects operational costs, logistics, and the ability to serve customers.

#### 15. **Technology and Necessary Tools**

- **Definition**: The technologies and tools used to support business operations, including software, hardware, and other technological resources.

- **Importance**: Essential for improving efficiency, productivity, and competitiveness.

#### 16. **Financial Projections**

- **Definition**: Future estimates of revenue,

expenses, and profits based on analysis and projections. Includes projected balance sheets, income statements, and cash flow forecasts.

- **Importance**: Helps to plan and manage financial resources and evaluate the sustainability and profitability of the company.

#### 17. **Budgeting and Cost Management**

- **Definition**: Planning and monitoring company expenses to ensure that the company stays within budget and optimizes costs.

- **Importance**: Crucial for financial control and maximizing profitability.

#### 18. **Break-Even Analysis**

- **Definition**: The evaluation of the sales level needed to cover all fixed and variable costs, to avoid losses.

- **Importance**: Helps determine profitability and plan pricing and sales strategies.

#### 19. **Financing and Investments**

- **Definition**: Financial resources obtained from external sources such as investors, bank loans, or venture capital, to finance company activities and growth.

- **Importance**: Fundamental for starting and expanding the company and supporting operations and development projects.

#### 20. **Risks and Mitigation**

- **Definition**: Identification of potential risks that could negatively impact the company and strategies to reduce or manage them.

- **Importance**: Helps to prepare for potential issues and minimize negative impacts on business results.

#### 21. **Emergency Plan**

- **Definition**: A detailed plan for addressing crisis or emergency situations, such as natural disasters, business interruptions, or financial problems.

- **Importance**: Essential for ensuring continuity of operations and company resilience in critical situations.

#### 22. **KPIs (Key Performance Indicators)**

- **Definition**: Metrics used to measure and evaluate business performance against set objectives. Examples include revenue, profit margin, and customer retention rate.

- **Importance**: Provide concrete data to monitor progress and make informed decisions.

#### 23. **Return on Investment (ROI)**

- **Definition**: A measure of the profitability of an investment, calculated as the ratio of net gain to initial investment.

- **Importance**: Helps to evaluate the effectiveness of investments and make decisions on further resource allocation.

#### 24. **Financial Projections**

- **Definition**: Future estimates of the company's financial performance based on historical data and assumptions. Includes revenue, expense, and profit forecasts.

- **Importance**: Fundamental for planning growth and attracting investors.

#### 25. **Capital Structure**

- **Definition**: The composition of the company's funding sources, including equity capital and debt capital.

- **Importance**: Influences financial risk and the company's ability to sustain operations and grow.

#### 26. **Marketing Plan**

- **Definition**: A strategic plan that defines the marketing activities and campaigns to promote the company's products or services.

- **Importance**: Essential for attracting customers and generating sales, and for positioning the company in the market.

#### 27. **Operational Plan**

- **Definition**: A detailed plan of the company's daily operations, including processes and resources needed to achieve business objectives.

- **Importance**: Guides daily activities and ensures that operations align with the business strategy.

#### 28. **Strategic Plan**

- **Definition**: A long-term plan that defines the company's strategic direction and the actions needed to achieve future objectives.

- **Importance**: Provides a vision and a roadmap for the company's future.

#### 29. **Product Life Cycle**

- **Definition**: The stages through which a product passes from its introduction to the market to its discontinuation. Includes introduction, growth, maturity, and decline.

- **Importance**: Helps to plan marketing and product management strategies throughout its life cycle.

#### 30. **Value Proposition**

- **Definition**: The statement that describes the unique value a product or service offers to customers and why they should choose it over the competition.

- **Importance**: Essential for differentiating the company's offering and attracting customers.

#### 31. **Performance Evaluation**

- **Definition**: The process of measuring and analyzing business performance against set objectives.

- **Importance**: Allows monitoring progress, identifying areas for improvement, and making strategic decisions.

#### 32. **Break-Even Point**

- **Definition**: The point where total revenue equals total costs, resulting in no profit or loss.

- **Importance**: Fundamental for determining the minimum sales level needed to cover costs and start generating profit.

#### 33. **Contingency Plan**

- **Definition**: A plan that provides alternative actions in case of unforeseen events or changes in market conditions.

- **Importance**: Helps to prepare and respond quickly to unexpected situations, minimizing negative impact.

#### 34. **Cash Flow**

- **Definition**: The movement of money in and out of the company, affecting its liquidity.

- **Importance**: Essential for ensuring the company has enough liquidity to operate and manage its financial obligations.

#### 35. **Working Capital**

- **Definition**: The difference between the company's current assets and current liabilities, indicating the availability of resources for daily operations.

- **Importance**: Crucial for managing operations and ensuring short-term solvency.

#### 36. **Leverage**

- **Definition**: The use of debt capital to increase the potential return on investments. Measured by the ratio of debt to equity.

- **Importance**: Can enhance returns but also increases financial risk.

#### 37. **Asset Management**

- **Definition**: The process of managing a company's assets to maximize their value and efficiency.

- **Importance**: Helps to optimize resource utilization and improve financial performance.

#### 38. **Human Resources (HR)**

- **Definition**: The management of personnel, including recruitment, training, performance evaluation, and employee relations.

- **Importance**: Essential for attracting, developing, and retaining talent, and for fostering a productive work environment.

#### 39. **Supply Chain Management**

- **Definition**: The management of the flow of goods and services from suppliers to customers, including procurement, production, and logistics.

- **Importance**: Crucial for ensuring timely delivery, cost efficiency, and quality of products and services.

#### 40. **Customer Relationship

Management (CRM)**

- **Definition**: Strategies and technologies used to manage interactions with customers and improve customer satisfaction and loyalty.

- **Importance**: Helps to understand customer needs, improve service, and increase retention.

#### 41. **Innovation**

- **Definition**: The process of developing new ideas, products, or processes that bring added value and differentiation to the company.

- **Importance**: Essential for maintaining competitiveness and driving growth.

#### 42. **Corporate Social Responsibility (CSR)**

- **Definition**: The company's commitment to operate ethically and contribute to economic development while improving the quality of life for its employees, community, and society.

- **Importance**: Enhances company reputation and creates positive social and environmental impacts.

#### 43. **Sustainability**

- **Definition**: The practice of operating in a way that meets current needs without compromising the ability of future generations to meet their own needs.

- **Importance**: Ensures long-term viability and aligns with increasing stakeholder expectations for responsible business practices.

#### 44. **Intellectual Property (IP)**

- **Definition**: Legal rights to inventions, designs, and artistic works that provide a competitive advantage.

- **Importance**: Protects innovations and helps to monetize intellectual assets.

#### 45. **Exit Strategy**

- **Definition**: A plan for how the company will be sold or transferred to new owners, or how investors will realize their return.

- **Importance**: Provides a roadmap for future transitions and helps to maximize value for owners and investors.

#### 46. **Growth Strategy**

- **Definition**: A plan for expanding the company's market share, product offerings, or geographic presence.

- **Importance**: Guides the company's efforts to increase revenue and scale operations.

#### 47. **Value Chain**

- **Definition**: The series of activities that add value to a company's products or services, from development to delivery.

- **Importance**: Helps to identify opportunities for optimization and value creation.

#### 48. **Benchmarking**

- **Definition**: The process of comparing a company's performance and processes to those of industry leaders or competitors.

- **Importance**: Helps to identify best practices and areas for improvement.

#### 49. **Brand Equity**

- **Definition**: The value of a company's brand based on consumer perception, recognition, and loyalty.

- **Importance**: Enhances competitive advantage and can increase market value.

#### 50. **Scalability**

- **Definition**: The ability of a business model or system to handle increased demand and growth without compromising performance.

- **Importance**: Ensures that the company

can grow efficiently and sustainably.

#### 51. **Product-Market Fit**

- **Definition**: The degree to which a product satisfies a strong market demand.

- **Importance**: Indicates potential for success and growth in the market.

#### 52. **Revenue Streams**

- **Definition**: The sources of income generated by the company, such as sales, subscriptions, and licensing.

- **Importance**: Diversification of revenue streams reduces risk and enhances financial stability.

#### 53. **Gross Margin**

- **Definition**: The difference between revenue and cost of goods sold, expressed as a percentage of revenue.

- **Importance**: Indicates the profitability

of core business activities and informs pricing and cost management strategies.

#### 54. **Customer Lifetime Value (CLV)**

- **Definition**: The total revenue expected from a customer over their entire relationship with the company.

- **Importance**: Helps to determine the value of customer acquisition and retention strategies.

#### 55. **Product Development Lifecycle**

- **Definition**: The stages through which a product goes from conception to market launch and beyond.

- **Importance**: Guides the process of innovation and product management, ensuring efficient development and successful market entry.

#### 56. **Digital Transformation**

- **Definition**: The integration of digital technologies into all areas of a business, fundamentally changing how it operates and delivers value.

- **Importance**: Enhances efficiency, competitiveness, and customer experience in the digital age.

#### 57. **Stakeholders**

- **Definition**: Individuals or groups that have an interest or stake in the company's performance and outcomes, such as employees, customers, investors, and suppliers.

- **Importance**: Understanding stakeholder needs and expectations is crucial for effective management and achieving business objectives.

Understanding and effectively utilizing these terms are fundamental for drafting, interpreting, and applying a business plan, ensuring a thorough and professional approach to business planning and strategy.

**Index**

1. Introduction pg.4

2. General Structure of a Business Plan pg.10

3. Market Analysis in the Business Plan pg.19

4. Business Strategy in the Business Plan pg.29

5. Operational Plan in the Business Plan pg.43

6. Financial Plan in the Business Plan pg.60

**7. Risks and Mitigation in the Business Plan pg.73**

**8. Drafting the Business Plan pg.90**

**9. Presenting the Business Plan pg.100**

**10. Monitoring and Revising the Business Plan pg.109**

**11. Practical Examples of Business Plans 119**

**12. Glossary of Key Terms in Business Planning pg.134**

www.ingramcontent.com/pod-product-compliance
Lightning Source LLC
Chambersburg PA
CBHW071923210526
45479CB00002B/536